RUMPELSTILTSKIN ILLUSIONS

Chris Tait

Copyright @Chris Tait 2023

Introduction

Chris Tait is a poet, playwright and spoken word artist from Shetland, living in Glasgow. She reads on the radio and at spoken word events across Scotland.

Her audio play "A Toon Built Apo Shenanigans" was recorded by actors at the Dibble Tree Theatre in Carnoustie through In motion theatre. The book was published with the help of the Edinburgh based company The Book Whisperers.

Events she has read at include the Granite Noir Crime Festival in Aberdeen the poem for which is included in this book.

Links:

"Literary Skulduggery" the poetry book

"A Toon Built Apo Shenanigans" is free to listen to on iTunes, Anchor, Spotify and Amazon and the book is on Amazon too.

YouTube: www.youtube.com/watch?v=6Cgql1j19lk

Three men in a tub - A poem inspired by a painting

Contents

A Wolf In Sheep's Skin 1

Fields Of Spun Gold 3

Pseudonymous Skeletons 4

The Bubbly Jock 6

The Pict's Field Of Parliament 8

A Prince's Kiss Made Him A Frog 9

The Castle With Caped Gnomes 11

Forty Shades Of Fiddler's Green 14

A Fiddler's Fate 16

Plum And Peacock's Heraldry 18

Deer In Kilts Served Whisky 20

The Angel And Demon's Chapel 22

Frog In The Throat 23

The Grey Granite Gnarled 24

A Wolf In Sheep's Skin

Peasants were offered a hansel
By a wolf in sheep's skin
With voodoo utensils
From Rumpelstiltskin

It was a poisoned apple
Seeds didn't grow in Eden
The watering can hobbled
The paddocks were Britain

The trees like bobbles
With chased leprechauns
People's lives were double
Turning to frogs at dawn

Lands riddled with marbles
Jesters and harlequins
Debts read like scrabble
The wolf at the door grinned

A town made of mustard
Jacks, knaves and maidens
Graffiti reads untoward
On the jail's bastions

Crossed snakes and ladders
Improvised by magicians
The city slipped its stature
With true superstitions

Cards in sleeves of gangsters
Graves of newspaper futons
Epitaphs of swagger
Bones fastened with buttons

Politicians are pranksters
Masks in clouds of cotton
Play monopoly with bankers
At the selfish giant's garden

Fields Of Spun Gold

Fields of spun gold
Where fence and styles buckle
Lands floured and rolled
By wheels, axe and sickle

The clouds catch colds
Winds tease and tickle
Hollow valley and folds
Grounds of cheese and pickle

Pierced with rabbit holes
Tortoise and hares hurtle
Scarecrow's stripped shoe soles
Scratch out paths in puzzles

Barns with beasts cheek by jowl
Gales must wear muzzles
They are hushed by moles
Through the weed tousles

Barns lidded with thatch
Are tap danced in drizzle
Skies lit with a match
Then fire swallowing guzzles

Pseudonymous Skeletons

Herded across Britain
With dog whistle blows
Cats slipped their kittens
News sent by witch's crows

Lions led by donkeys
Through the miles of traps
Recruited like monkeys
Blindfolded with blood taps

Tanks trudging tandems
In the slippered frost
Fog puffs of phantoms
A canvas of ghosts

Cold acres of cotton
They staggered in snow
With threadbare mittens
And snowmen's toes

Gardens of guillotines
Soldier scarecrows stalked
Helter skelter mountains
Amputees piggy backed

Pseudonymous skeletons
Needles in haystacks
Angels fired as guardians
Men lost their way back

Comrades are buried
A three legged race
Mud and swamp ferried
Limbs pinned in a brace

The Bubbly Jock

A bubbly jock steered Noah's ark
To the isle of Whalsay
With cacophonies of barks
The trip was argy-bargy

He pulled out the bottle's corks
The genie language from Norway
And gathered it up with pitchforks
While shadows lurked in doorways

People who broadcast his mail
Spied on him like eagles
He overturned the yards of kale
Entertainment was the seagulls

The bubbly jock carried zodiacs
The devil's poetry
In a crow's cul-de-sac
Chickens ran the country

Gales in whirligigs
Saxophone chimneys
Rain like slovenly swigs
Names from bogus histories

He scoured the dialects
Witch hats held universities
Words he tried to protect
From the hurly-burly

In torrents of consciousness
Geese were his contemporary
With pasts mapped from a guess
He still ignites controversy

The Pict's Field Of Parliament

The Pict's field of parliament
Bogus, Bunce and Bean in a tent
Courtyards of ancient residents
Pickpocketing paid the rent

Scrooge's quotes as a testament
Freckles of decimal points
Balancing crofts on elephants
From circuses and horn hunts

Kings and queens were the parents
Who passed tools since they were flint
Found in rusting thimble hunts
Pirate's treasure was the mint

Guessing with dice to count
Reads of deeds in legal chants
Greensleeves's parks of plants
Where the horse and ploughman haunt

The round table and the tenants
Dwellings for priests, souls and saints
Still shadowed by their descendants
Spilling recipes in drops of paint

A Prince's Kiss Made Him A Frog

A horned ship with a tail tether
A figurehead's forked tongue
Sails courted by the rudder
A fiddle tightly strung

The plans were tongue twisters
From frying pans and into fires
Winds blustering feather dusters
Crews of a captain and squires

The Arctic measured in shovels
Food chains carried in jars
Storms caused seamen to grovel
They circled winking stars

Following the pied piper
To the ice like crosswords
Across oceans of copper
Scrubbed decks and jigs with swords

Salt over shoulders in circuits
As they ventured very far
Weathers pushed liners to fidget
Scraping through a mirror

Far out of reach Eden
It hid from binoculars
Mermaids at the garden
Who lured men to the polars

Provisions were tins of biscuits
Bitten by rancid vermin
Treacle scones from skies of thickets
Ducking apples in basins

Trips with the passing batons
Knowledge from a drowned face
Who tried the same mission
But couldn't win the race

Sleeping with rats on cushions
Shivering in scarecrow's rags
Grain as sealed barrel rations
A prince's kiss made him a frog

The Castle With Caped Gnomes

People slept with garlic
Echoing ouija
They delivered doric
A north sea opera

Pin pricked blood was toxic
Arteries in the taverns
Cliffs dribbled gin and tonic
Ice cubicles of caverns

The waves were hypnotic
Men clung to metronomes
The gulls were super sonic
The castle with caped gnomes

Thrown out a stone punnet
Then stuck in wood worm wheels
Brazen bees in bonnets
Rhythms of loathsome reels

Bagpiped wind hurled crotchets
Are what knitting needles clicked
Latches smashed with hatchets
The seals were so sea sick

The crofts were crocheted
Mermaids carried in the creels
Crosses crushed by mallets
Grinding glockenspiels

Costume balls so chaotic
Horns under hats revealed
Windows with cataracts
Cobwebbed woven meals

Fisherfolk were robotic
Banquets stacked like stairs
The plankton was bionic
Escaping nets from tears

Through hoops so hectic
The Tam O'Shanter path
The seabed was septic
A warlock filled bath

Rocks of tonsil and gromit
Jaws of legend bears
Gargling lava to vomit
Atlantis's layer

Dust freckled candlesticks
Tackled three blind mice
Lighting matches in licks
Then scurried like a dice

Scorpions were transport
Ship's portholes spied the pit
Cliffs with lesions and warts
Season's epileptic fits

An upset apple cart
Fares were paid in stings
Aries the ewe at the marts
Whales waited in the wings

Dracula's iron fangs
Drunk blood from razored necks
His pickled body hung
He rose from fastened sacks

Nailed in crate and box coffins
Knotted with a sash
With turrets of muffins
The building had a rash

The seas like carousels
A bucking bronco horse
Schizophrenic door bells
A widdershin course

Vampires climbed totem poles
To gatekeepers on a noose
Entered castles through holes
Spiral steps in a sluice

A demon on his deathbed
Handed them keys to locked rooms
Grids for a blanket spread
Body snatchers poked a tomb

Forty Shades Of Fiddler's Green

Men kidnapped by a submarine
Told from a message in a bottle
Seas forty shades of fiddler's green
So deep they touched the fossils

They had spindrift in their genes
Stalwart like the thistles
Departed kingdoms to their queens
Diamonds were spliced to drizzle

Fish addressed from the ravine
And delivered letters
Opera of wives and daughter's keen (whails)
Men transformed to lobsters

Vandals who snapped a wishbone
Cowboys disrupted otters
The ocean would now be their throne
Dolphins were the butlers

The step sons of Neptune
They became shackled brothers
A lighthouse turned hot air balloon
They were all tipped over

At the solitary isle
No happy ever after
Or bearing from a sundial
Oilskins hung on cloud rafters

In the belly of a whale
Scripture from narrators
Bedtime stories, nightmare tales
With cues and clues on ledgers

Written on a strip of sail
Truths from bottomless craters
With the water needing bailed
Angel's lifeboats were stretchers

A Fiddler's Fate

A troubadour and slave
Caught a random train
Jamming with the climate's rave
And the windmills of rain

Squeezed in an outlawed cave
Through tunnels shrunk to drains
Over lost traveller's graves
On the edge of a plain

He struck up tunes with his pipes
Which echoed reels in reverse
The sea swelled with salted swipes
Warning of a fairy's curse

Runes read not to be disturbed
Or they would take revenge
With steam punk spikes and barbs
For his bed he'd have to scrounge

They would make him scrub the den
Like a chimney sweep
Portraits hung of vanished men
They haunted him in sleep

They accompanied him as crew
Then suffered a fiddler's fate
Of falling in pots of brew
Their teeth chattered in grates

He scaled a brush to a painting
Past Billy goats gruff to land
Trolls under the bridge's ranting
Slipping vanilla sands

With fairies complaining
Pictures were thrown in the fires
The friends were acquainting
Men climbed up pans on meat stairs

And fairies sleeping and yawning
Their eyes flashing as strobes
Men paid them stones for renting
Fairies chased pipes on tightropes

Plum And Peacock's Heraldry

Orphans ran to join the circus
With floorboards like monopoly
Pirate stations on a wireless
Transmitted from an imp's laundry

With the three witch's chorus
The margins of Jackanory
Statues were chivalrous
Clown's eyes were strawberries

In a monocle's focus
Scotland with moats of sherry
Distilled by an angel's purpose
Tribal dances in cemeteries

The ruins reeled so raucous
Rockets popped from chimneys
Fiddler's bids as a bonus
Axed doors leaked out zombies

Skeletons twirled on a harness
In ball gowns patched and gory
Heeled and toed in fungus
Plum and Peacock's heraldry

Guests tucked in bed at forests
Didgeridoos puffed air in glass
Beasts packed horns into a suitcase
Compensations reclaimed with brass

Palm readings on mermaid's hands
Maypoles with eels at stream's ribbons
Bodhran scored, seal sung islands
Picts hid in caves like goblins

Deer In Kilts Served Whisky

Tapestries of loose ends
Hooked ones who shared laughter
Farewell vigils with friends
For happy ever after

Approaching the milestone stop
To begin the next chapter
Shinty with brooms and mops
Their bubbled path crossed borders

From hijacked books folk read
Footnotes scratched the surface
With flames of marmalade
Longships scorched in a furnace

The crystal tears did baptise
Gold forged from cups of tea
A cuckoo clock surprise
Deer in kilts served whisky

The drifting kite Saltire skies
With fish and sheep currency
Alba's lilting lullabies
A grouse scribed as secretary

The blood's viking ties
Noah herded across the sea
Sailing sunken sailor's cries
Peat torches made blacksmith's keys

The fried eggs of sunrise
Shells broke like humpty dumpty
Over Scotland's plaid hung knees
Clothes washed in burns by banshees

Weather forecasts of sugar and spice
Alarms were cockledoodle do
Sea monsters lingered in the ice
Pub banter from well oiled crews

The Angel And Demon's Chapel

The angel and demon's chapel
Built with spoons and syrup
And Adam and Eve's apple
The garden grew from that pip

There is a whispered fable
A grail in a lucky dip
Blind man's bluff in the bible
Could be hidden behind a lip

The letters would be cripple
The grounds might be stripped
Ventriloquist apostles
Or a fist's iron grip

Details that game gobble
Dangled in smattered nips
Pyramids of rubble
Flashes of newspaper clips

The toppled tower of Babel
Could provide a tip
Under structures which crumble
The bloodline would drip

Shelves which wiggle and wobble
Artefacts cracked, creased and chipped
An heirloom crucible
In an out of reach crypt

Frog In The Throat

From Atlantis's Aladdin's caves
The fish that never swam surfaced
And mermaids with harp laden waves
Pisces coat of arm's service

He held the ring behind his fin
It was golden like the harvest
Over the farm's feathered chin
Metamorphosed to varnish

He eclipsed a tangled net
A coiled and frayed jewelled necklace
Wound round him in the corked bands
A shark was a smirking menace

Halos rose from dripping loops
Seas were musical chair furnished
Octopus in cask spilled scoops
Stained glass windows Sinbad polished

The Grey Granite Gnarled

The city's underworld
Fraudsters and fugitives
The grey granite gnarled
Secrets whispered to graves

Of the bludgeoned and poisoned
The jail doors are slammed
After being questioned
Cells are tightly crammed

The crooks locked in prisons
With smudged fingerprints
And criminals partitioned
Had a sentence to count

Some escaped in missions
Where the scoundrels haunt
In a state of concussion
From concealed outlawed joints

In bunkers and burrows
A rummage by the sleuths
Streets and closes so narrow
Trap doors to toll booths

Rows were flung arrows
Some lost eyes, toes and a tooth
Stashes smuggled in marrows
Cued treasure hunts for the truth

Magnifying glass windows
Spiked whiskey and rum
Strangers in shadows
With gloved fingers and thumbs

All the witches were burned
With courts holding victims
The convicts were warned
Cautioned culprits and hoodlums

Clues police followed
Listening to the humdrum
Trees were used as gallows
Bodies hung like plums

In a shrivelled meadow
Corpses were so glum
Leaving grieving widows
Penniless and numb

Printed in Great Britain
by Amazon